_____

Presented To

_____

Presented By

_____

Date

Twenty-Three Power Scriptures to Overcome Adversities

Speaking God's Word to Today's Adversities

RON COBBS

WESTBOW
PRESS®
A DIVISION OF THOMAS NELSON
& ZONDERVAN

Copyright © 2023 Ron Cobbs.

All rights reserved. No part of this book may be used or reproduced by any means, graphic, electronic, or mechanical, including photocopying, recording, taping or by any information storage retrieval system without the written permission of the author except in the case of brief quotations embodied in critical articles and reviews.

This book is a work of non-fiction. Unless otherwise noted, the author and the publisher make no explicit guarantees as to the accuracy of the information contained in this book and in some cases, names of people and places have been altered to protect their privacy.

WestBow Press books may be ordered through booksellers or by contacting:

WestBow Press
A Division of Thomas Nelson & Zondervan
1663 Liberty Drive
Bloomington, IN 47403
www.westbowpress.com
844-714-3454

Because of the dynamic nature of the Internet, any web addresses or links contained in this book may have changed since publication and may no longer be valid. The views expressed in this work are solely those of the author and do not necessarily reflect the views of the publisher, and the publisher hereby disclaims any responsibility for them.

Any people depicted in stock imagery provided by Pexels Images are models, and such images are being used for illustrative purposes only.

Interior Image Credit: Pexel (https://pexels.com/license), Ron Cobbs

ISBN: 979-8-3850-0069-2 (sc)
ISBN: 979-8-3850-0070-8 (hc)
ISBN: 979-8-3850-0071-5 (e)

Library of Congress Control Number: 2023910897

Printed in the United States of America.

WestBow Press rev. date: 09/01/2023

Scripture quotations marked (KJV) are taken from King James version of the Bible, public domain.

Scripture quotations marked (NKJV) are taken from the New King James Version. Copyright © 1982 by Thomas Nelson, Inc. Used by permission. All rights reserved.

Scriptures marked NLT are taken from the Holy Bible, New Living Translation, copyright © 1996, 2004, 2015 by Tyndale House Foundation. Used by permission of Tyndale House Publishers Inc., Carol Stream, Illinois 60188. All rights reserved.

Introduction

Have you ever wondered, *Lord, I can't take no more! Why am I in this mess? What am I going to do? How do I get through this impossible scenario?* This COVID-19 pandemic doesn't look like it is going to end! Gasoline prices are skyrocketing, and my salary isn't matching the cost-of-living increases!

I know how you feel. I *know* how you feel! When all these circumstances are just piling up, it seems like God isn't listening. And you feel all alone. A couple of years ago, these thoughts were flowing through my mind. I started a new position at my job and was feeling as though I didn't know anything, nor did I know what to do.

Well, let me share something with you. You are *exactly* where God wants you to be. I know you're thinking, *Ron, that doesn't make sense! You mean to tell me that God is allowing all these things to happen to me?* Guess what. If God is allowing it, then there is a reason. It could be something that *you* have done in the past of which you are reaping the harvest of the bad seed that was planted. But that doesn't mean that it is over. It could be the enemy attacking you trying to prevent you from doing God's will. Again, there is a reason why. Here is the key:

God will allow things to happen to you
so that you *must* depend on *Him!*

It is common human nature for us to want to do things independently on our own, thinking that it was all of us and we don't need God. Remember that when Moses led the children of Israel through the wilderness, they were complaining about food. And God gave them manna (bread from heaven). For forty years, God provided manna every morning, and the people went out to pick it up. But here is the key: they were *only* allowed to get enough for their family for *one* day. If they tried to gather more, then it would spoil. Why did God do this? He was training them to depend on *Him* daily!

So now, getting back to the issues that you are facing. I learned that I must depend on Him daily. I learned to speak His Word (Rhema) over my situation because His Word never comes back void. When you speak verbally His written Word, something powerful happens!

Although there are thousands of scriptures in the Bible, I found twenty-three power scriptures that have knocked down barriers, opened closed doors, and created peace that was beyond what I can understand.

I pray and believe that if you say out loud these scriptures daily, you will begin to see an increase in your faith and see God start working in your daily life!

Be tremendously blessed!

Ron Cobbs

How to Read This Book

The purpose of this book is to guide you through twenty-three powerful scriptures that you can use to not only read but also to commit to memory so that you can recall and say them out loud in times of crisis and in times of tranquility. Never wait until the storm starts before you start to prepare yourself for the storm. Preparing for adversity always starts when things are peaceful, when the sun is shining, and when things are good. Reading these scriptures and quoting them out loud daily is the preparing part. Over time, you will be amazed how when a crisis pops up, a scripture will come to mind. Speaking the scripture out loud informs the enemy that God's Word is stronger than your environment. Speaking the scriptures out loud is basically speaking God's Word, not *your* words, over the circumstances. Speaking God's Word activates His supreme authority and sovereignty because God's words will not return to Him void and empty.

This book is designed into the following parts:

- reading the scriptures (God's Word)
- reading the thoughts/story that corresponds to the scriptures

- speaking out loud the scriptures so that your physical ears can hear it and your spiritual ears can receive it
- memorizing the scriptures and storing them in your spiritual arsenal so that the Holy Spirit can bring them to your memory at the time that you need it the most

You may say, "I'm not good at memorizing" or "I hate to memorize things." The intent is not to just memorize scripture. Memorizing is just a function of the brain. The goal is to memorize and make the scriptures a part of your life. When you get to the scripture that says, "Thy Word have I hidden in my heart so that I would not sin against thee," you can personalize it by saying, "Dear Heavenly Father, I am purposely reading, memorizing, and making Your Word hidden in my spirit so that I will not fall short and commit a sin against Your Word."

As you read each scripture, ask God, "What are You saying to me, and what does it really mean? How will I be able to use this scripture in the future?" Finally, ask God as you read the scripture to help you to remember them in time of need.

Picture by Scott Santa Maria, Pexels.

1

When you go through deep waters, I will be with you. When you go through rivers of difficulty, you will not drown. When you walk through the fire of oppression, you will not be burned up; the flames will not consume you.
—Isaiah 43:2 (NLT)

There isn't a day that goes by when you do not feel like you are struggling to get things done or struggling to figure things out on your own. Sometimes you wonder, *Why, God, is this happening to me? Why now in my life? It is not fair that I should be the only one experiencing this!* And the biggest fear or emotional hurt that we go through is that no one around us understands what we are going through. How many times have you tried to tell someone your fears or pain and suddenly that person is talking about what they went through and the whole topic is on them? It is very common that the person you are talking to ends up sharing what they went through in their efforts to let you know that *they* know what you are going through. Well, that may be all true. But when you are hurt, afraid, angry, upset, confused, etc., sometimes you just need a friend to listen to you. Someone to just be there for you. Someone who will not interrupt you while trying to get their story in or get their point across.

Well, guess what. God knows you, understands you, is patient enough to listen to you, and is with you. He promises never to leave or forsake you. You are the apple of His eye. He has *your* name written in the palm of His hand. I recently learned that the palm of your hand is the most painful place to get a tattoo. Also, the skin cells in the palm of your hand have the most rapid skin growth. This means that every couple of years, you have to do a retouch of the tattoo because the tattoo will fade away. God has your name written in the palm of His hand, and it will never fade away.

When you are afraid and feel that you are alone, remember that you are not alone. God will go through the fire with you just like He did with the three Hebrew boys who were thrown in the fiery furnace. God wants you to trust in Him, even when you can't see Him, touch Him, or feel Him. He is there! He is there!

Picture by Ron Cobbs.

2

For the Lord gives wisdom; From His mouth comes knowledge and understanding.
—Proverbs 2:6 (NKJV)

There are two kinds of wisdom: man's wisdom and God's wisdom. Man's wisdom only comes from experience (going through things, making mistakes, learning from the mistakes, and learning not to do them again). Also, you can take advice from another person, but trust me: they got that wisdom from someone else or from going through it themselves, making their mistakes, learning from the mistakes, and learning not to do them again. In fact, you will always hear them say, "Hey, if I were you, I wouldn't do that because …" Here is the downside of man's wisdom: Sometimes it takes a long time to learn the lesson. (That is time away from your life!) And sometimes the mistakes you make will be stuck with you for the rest of your life. I'm not saying that you will not move forward in life. I'm just saying that mistakes can cause you to feel shame or prevent you from being at the level sooner or quicker than you had hoped to be. How many folks can think back on a couple of mistakes they made and wish they had never done them? You are wiser now. But still you wish that you hadn't done the mistakes.

God's wisdom is unique because no person, no angel, and no demon can match the wisdom that God has. God used wisdom to create and prepare the heavens. (See Proverbs 8:27.) Wisdom is an important thing to have. Why? Because God's wisdom gives you insight and knowledge about things without you having to endure the heartache of going through a painful mistake that will cost you time or—even worse—character.

The definition of *wisdom* is the application of knowledge. I know a lot of people who are full of facts and information but have no insight in how to apply the knowledge to make the right decisions for their lives. There are folks who are "walking Wikipedias" of information but make poor decisions with money or their lives.

The same wisdom that God used to establish the foundations of the earth is available to you. All you have to do is ask Him, and He will freely give it to you. (See James 1:5.)

Picture by M. Venter, Pexels.

3

**You will not need to fight in this battle. Position yourselves, stand still and see the salvation of the Lord.
—2 Chronicles 20:17 (NKJV)**

There are two types of battles that we fight: physical and spiritual.

1. Physical battles are when the enemy comes to attack you, take possession of your land, property, and territory, and destroy all the works that you've done. This is the same as a country going to war against another country or if you have a terrible neighbor who seeks to destroy your property because they don't like you. Physical battles can also be attacks against your body that make you sick.
2. Spiritual battles are when the battlefield resides in your mind. These battles have the same objective of destroying you, and the enemy uses lying thoughts that are contrary to what God's Word says. If you are not deeply engrossed in God's Word, then the enemy can throw partial truths to your mind and you begin to question or doubt God's Word. Remember how Eve was tricked by Satan in the Garden of Eden because he got her to question what God had already said? It is like a true-and-false question that you get on an exam in school. Ninety-nine percent of the statement can be true, but one word that is not true will make the whole statement false. Think about that!

So why does God allow battles to come to you? Because He wants you to *seek Him* and *trust Him*. The scripture 2 Chronicles 20:17

tells a powerful story of how the people of Moab, the people of Ammon, and others (a total of three armies) decided to wage war against the children of Israel. The people of Israel (tribe of Judah) ran to King Jehoshaphat, telling him that a great multitude of people were coming against them (from Syria) from beyond the sea. In fact, the armies were already at the location of En Gedi, which is fifty-four miles (86.3 kilometers) from Jerusalem. King Jehoshaphat did something very powerful and very simple. He stood in the assembly of the tribe of Judah and prayed out loud, asking God for help. When he finished his prayer, the prophet Jahaziel stood up in the midst of the assembly and said, "Thus says the Lord to you ..." When you pray an earnest and honest prayer to God, He hears you and He will answer.

Jesus said in this world you will have tribulation. Jesus never said that from now on, it is going to be the smoothest, easiest, most trouble-free life you will ever have. No! He told His disciples, and He is telling us, that in life we *will* encounter troubles, tribulation, and battles. But you are not alone. The battles that you encounter are never planned for you to fight alone. They are planned for you to seek God. He will fight the battles for you so that you will *know* that He is sovereign and omnipotent and cares for you!

Picture by Pexels, Pixabay.

4

**I can do all things through Christ who strengthens me.
—Philippians 4:13 (NKJV)**

What a power statement apostle Paul wrote while he was under house arrest in Rome. Paul sent a letter (epistle) to the church that was started in the small city of Philippi around the years AD 60–62. While under house arrest, he was in chains twenty-four hours a day, seven days a week. But despite his imprisonment, Paul reaches out to them with words of encouragement. Two women (Euodia and Syntyche) had started the small church in Philippi, but over time, the church started to come across discord.

In the midst of the discord, Paul emphasizes the importance of unity and being of the same like-mindedness. Then he begins to specifically target what our minds need to concentrate on (i.e., rejoicing in the Lord and being anxious for nothing, and in everything focusing on prayer and supplication).

As profound a statement as "I can do all things through Christ who strengthens me," sometimes the human emotions do not catch up to what you just read. It is hard to feel victorious when everything you see around you is crumbling down. Here is the key: Get your eyes off yourself and focus on the Lord Jesus Christ! Jesus was very clear when He spoke to His disciples, telling them that without Him, you can do nothing. (See John 15:5.)

Frustration is trying to do things on your own without God. The moment you realize that you can't do everything on your own, you humble yourself in the presence of God and tell Him that you need Him. *That* is when He steps into your life to make things happen.

Picture by Pexels, Pixabay.

5

Count it all joy when you fall into various trials and tribulation, knowing that the testing of your faith produces patience.
—Philippians 4:13 (NKJV)

I have heard this scripture preached by many pastors in my life. When I was going through struggles, I hated to hear this scripture because I felt like the person speaking didn't know what I was going through. They were just saying the "Christianly" words to sound holy. It is very easy to say to someone else, "Count all joy when you fall into various trials," but it is hard to remember this scripture while you are going through the trials.

For years I was missing a major point in this scripture that didn't allow me to have joy. James wrote, "If you know this, then you will be able to count any trial that you are experiencing as joy." Here it is, "knowing that the testing of your faith produces patience." I must borrow something that I learned from a great teacher named Dr. Fredrick K. C. Price. Notice that the trial test isn't about you. *It is the testing your faith!* John wrote (1 John 5:4) that it is our faith that overcomes the world. If the enemy can get you to faulter in your faith, then he has won. But if you stand strong in your faith, the trial that you are going through produces even more patience. God is the one who gives you strength to endure.

I used to wonder why God allows the trials to come to my life. The answer is simple. There is a reason. God always has a plan and reason why He allows the trials to enter your life. The answer has two parts: so that you get closer to Him and so that He can use the situation to show that He is sovereign and when He pulls you through the trial, others will see that God is working in your life. When Lazarus of Bethany was very sick, Mary (the same woman who anointed Jesus's feet with fragrant oil and wiped His feet with her hair) and Martha (Mary's sister) sent for Jesus so that He could heal Lazarus. When Jesus heard that Lazarus was sick, He said, "This sickness is not unto death, but for the glory of God" (John 11:4). Jesus was telling others that this bad event is not for us to focus on just the bad event. The entire event was used to show others that Jesus is the resurrection and the life and that you believe who Jesus is.

Trials are opportunities for God to do a mighty work through you so that others who see you can believe that God is real, and their hearts will be changed to want to become believers in Jesus Christ. Remember the trial that you are going through is not a test against you. It is testing your faith.

Picture by Ingo Joseph, Pexels.

6

Oh (Lord[1]), that You would bless me indeed and enlarge my territory, that Your hand would be with me, and that you would keep me from evil, that I might not cause pain.
—1 Chronicles 4:10 (NKJV)

This is a very bold prayer that Jabez prayed to God. I can imagine Jabez's mother telling him, "The reason why I gave you the name Jabez is because it was very painful while I gave birth to you." What mother tells their child that they were a pain to them? All mothers who give birth in pain experience something immediately after birth called endorphins and happiness when they see their baby. But this mother from the beginning didn't want her child. The only thing that she says to her son is that he was a pain to her. How many other children go through rejection from their parents? The answer is *a lot*.

The Bible doesn't talk that much about Jabez, but it does mention that Jabez was more honorable than his brothers. In spite of the rejection he received from his mother, he still did the right thing that was honorable in the sight of the Lord. I can imagine him feeling lonely and just wanting to feel loved by someone. Jabez was probably feeling very down, yet he still knew there was a God. Jabez was a descendant in the family from the tribe of Judah, which is one of the twelve brothers from the father Jacob (Israel).

---

[1] NKJV excludes "Lord."

In the middle of his loneliness, Jabez still had dreams and desires similar to what we have today. Jabez boldly asked God for these five things:

1. to bless him
2. to enlarge his territory
3. to be with him (protection)
4. to keep him from evil (guidance)
5. to prevent him from causing harm to others

Most Christians only ask God for the first two and never add the remaining three items. God doesn't mind you having stuff as long as the stuff doesn't get in the way of you serving Him, the stuff leads you down the path of evil, and the stuff causes you to be cruel to others. Remember Jesus said that if you abide (live with) Him, and His Word abides in you, you can ask whatever you want, and it will be done for you (John 15:7).

God is a loving God and He cares for you. When God blesses you, it is because He loves you and He wants you to use His blessings to help someone else. Why? So that others will believe there is a God and their hearts will be changed to want to follow Him.

Picture by Ryutaro Tsukata, Pexels.

7

But if the same Spirit of Him who raised Jesus from the dead dwells in you, He who raised Christ from the dead will also give life to your mortal bodies through His Spirit who dwells in you.
—Romans 8:11 (NKJV)

One day while I was walking/jogging in the park, I said to the Lord, "God, when I get to heaven, I can't wait to talk to some of the prophets or some of the people that I've read in the Old Testament. For example, I would love to ask Moses, "What was like to be on Mt. Sinai with God and hearing Him speak to you and seeing Him write the Ten Commandments on the tablets of stone?" The children of Israel were at the bottom of the mountain all afraid because what they saw on Mt. Sinai was terrifying. When God spoke, the whole mountain shook! God came down upon the mountain and there was smoke. God's voice sounded like a loud blast of trumpets! Also on the same mountain, Moses asked God if he could see Him. So God said, "OK, but you can't see My face." God told Moses to stand by this rock, and when His glory passes by, God will cover his face with His hands and only allow Moses to see His back. Well, guess what happened? When Moses saw God's back, the power of God's glory was so overwhelming that He started worshipping the Lord. When Moses came down from Mt. Sinai, his face was shining so brightly that the children of Israel couldn't look at Moses's face. They were terrified and Moses had to veil his face.

There are many other characters that we've read in the Bible who are in heaven now, but I had to share that story of Moses to give an idea of the relationship that God had with His people. This is the awesome God who created the heavens, the earth, every creature, and even man in just six days. This is the sovereign being of which there is no other God like Jehovah! No one can compare to Him.

So guess what God said to me when I mentioned to Him about Moses and the other characters. God said, "Guess what Moses and the other characters will ask you? When you ask your question, they will say, 'Yes, it was an amazing and awesome sight to see all the things that God did, but tell us what it was like to have God (the most powerful being of which no other creature can compare) living inside of you?' Did God part the Atlantic Ocean for you? What miracles did you perform? How many thousands of souls did you preach to and saw their lives changed?" I literally stopped jogging in the park. I'm talking literally stopped in my tracks. Then God said, "You really don't know the depth of what we did and the sacrifice Jesus made on the cross. When Jesus died on the cross and the veil of the temple was torn, we moved the Holy of Holies from a building to a living building (human body) because we love you so much! We (God, Jesus, and the Holy Spirit) want to be with you and live inside of you. You have so much more than what Moses had because the closest we could get to them was in a tent in the Holy of Holies. Now the scriptures—1 Corinthian 6:19 "Your body is the temple of the Spirit" and 1 John 4:4 "Greater is He who is IN you, than he who is in the world"—have a deeper meaning. If you are a believer in Jesus Christ and have accepted Him to live inside of you, then you have the one who has created the universe living inside of you. Completely mind-boggling yet comforting.

Picture by Yuri Laymin, Pexels.

8

Behold, I give you[2] the authority to trample on serpents and scorpions, and over all the power of the enemy, and nothing shall by any means hurt you.
—Luke 10:19 (NKJV)

It is clear by now you are starting to notice that I start each section with saying, "What a powerful scripture!" Or something similar. But this scripture is really unique.

To place in context, Jesus had just given power to His twelve disciples to have authority over all demons, to cure diseases, to heal the sick, and to preach the kingdom of God (Luke 9:1–6). When the disciples came back, they noticed there was a large crowd of people hanging around and following them. The disciples tried to send the crowd away because they were concerned about not having food to feed them. But Jesus performed a miracle and caused five loaves of bread and two fish to multiply and fed the five thousand families. Jesus was demonstrating the power of the Holy Spirit to not only cast out demons and heal the sick, but the Holy Spirit will be *what* you need *when* you need it.

So after the miracle of feeding the five thousand people, Jesus revealed who He really was to just three disciples (Peter, John, and James) when on top of a mountain; His face began to shine as brightly as the sun. And His robe was white and glistening (Luke 9:29). Next, Elijah and Moses appeared and started talking to

---

[2] NKJV excludes "power and."

Jesus. (Hang on. I'm getting there. Just setting up the uniqueness of Luke 10:19.)

After the power event on top of a mountain, more people approached Jesus saying that they wanted to follow Him. But Jesus explained to them the cost of discipleship. Then Jesus appointed seventy more people and sent them out to do the same things that the twelve disciples did (i.e., cast out demons, cure diseases, heal the sick, and preach the kingdom of God; Luke 10:1–12). When the people returned, they were so full of joy, saying, "Lord, even the demons are subject to us in your name." Here is the kicker: Jesus responded to them, "I saw Satan fall like lightning from heaven." That is past tense, meaning, He was there before the Garden of Eden and saw when Satan rebelled against God, getting kicked out of heaven. Here is something else. When Jesus was in the wilderness being tempted by Satan, Satan told Jesus that if He worshipped him, He would give Him all the kingdoms of the world because they were given to him. At that time, Satan had the authority. But now, Jesus is saying, "I have the authority!" This was before Jesus even died on the cross!

Jesus pointed out in Luke 9:49 that His power is not just for the disciples. It is for anyone who believes. Anything is possible to him who believes in Jesus.

Picture by Ron Cobbs.

9

**As thy day is, so shall thy strength be.
—Deuteronomy 33:25 (KJV)**

As we get older, there are many times when we will ask God, "Lord, when will it get easier? I'm tired of struggling. I'm tired of pushing and pressing only to get knocked down by others or circumstances and events. Lord, I'm tired and sometimes I just want to close my eyes and everything just goes away."

God knows exactly how you feel. He does! In fact, the scripture says that we have someone (Jesus) who sympathizes with our weaknesses (Hebrews 4:15). So if God knows how we feel, and knows what we are going through, why does He allow it? God wants you to depend on Him daily. Not just come to Him one time, get everything you need at one sitting, then never return to Him for anything else. God seeks a personal relationship with you. He is not a genie in a bottle that you can just rub on the bottle, then *poof* out pops God saying, "What is your bidding?"

As the children of Israel were wandering in the wilderness, God fed them manna (bread from heaven). But he told them to only get enough that they need for that day. Every morning, the Israelites saw manna scattered everywhere on the ground. There were 2 million Israelites in the desert, so can you imagine the amount of manna that was on the ground? If they gathered more than what they needed for that day, the manna would spoil. So why would God do this to them? Because He gives you exactly what you need for that day, and He wants you to depend on Him for your needs.

When you wake up in the morning wondering how you are going to survive or get through the day, you need to remember to go to God and ask Him for what you need. He wants you to ask. Satan will put a thought in your mind, saying, "Aren't you tired of asking God for things? Doesn't God already know what you need? So why doesn't He just already do it for you?" You see, God does know all of your needs before you even ask Him. But He still wants you to ask. Why? Because He wants to be near you. He wants a relationship with you. He wants you to know that He is your provider and can do anything more than you can ever ask or think. He loves you that much!

Jesus reminded us in the ideal Lord's Prayer, "Give us this day our daily bread." He didn't tell us to ask God, "Give us all the bread and everything that we will ever need for the rest of our lives so that we don't have to bother you every day." We need to trust in the Lord for the strength that He provides for us *each* day. Each day we have everything we need to function and do what we need to do through Him.

Picture by Eberhard Grossgasteig, Pexels.

10

**The memory of the righteous is blessed.
—Proverbs 10:7 (NKJV)**

I have to confess that for years I have used this scripture for a totally different reason. When I finally looked up the background and meaning of this scripture, it gave me a different perspective. But God still helped me to apply this to my life today.

When I was in college, I would study hard for my exams. On the day of my exams, I would say this prayer: "The memory of the righteous is blessed." In other words, I was praying to God that He would help me to remember whatever I studied so that I could do well on the test. After looking up the word *memory* in Hebrew, I learned that it is the word *zeker,* which means "memorial remembrance." The righteous memorial is blessed, but the memorial of the wicked will rot.

So I asked the Lord, "How does this apply to me?" The response was quite easy and direct. Live your life in a righteous way, and God will bless your life while you are alive, and after you have passed away, others will remember your life that will be a blessing to them. Living righteously is not to be confused with the requirements of getting into heaven. We are saved and made righteous by grace (God's decision to give us what we don't deserve) based on what Jesus did. Not what we have done. There is no work that we could ever do (alone) to be considered righteous enough to get into heaven. Jesus did the heavy lifting by paying for our sin once and for all. So all that we need to do is accept God's free gift of salvation and redemption.

Now after we receive God's gift of accepting Jesus into our lives, we commission ourselves to learn everything about Jesus and do righteous things for Him. We are doing these righteous things to spread God's love to others and letting them know that He loves them too and wants them to be in heaven with the rest of the family.

Your righteous deeds store up treasures in heaven, but the act of kindness is for others here on this earth. When you act with the right motive, which is love (1 Corinthians 13), then God blesses your actions and your actions will be remembered. So be a blessing to someone. They need it.

Picture by Philippe Donn, Pexels.

11

Trust in the Lord with All of your heart and lean not to your own understanding. In all your ways, acknowledge Him and He will direct your paths.
—Proverbs 3:5-6 (NKJV)

This is probably one of the hardest scriptures to do. How do you trust a God that you can't see, can't audibly hear with your ears, can't physically feel with your hands, or even smell His presence? We live in a world of "Show me and I will believe." But God is saying, "Believe Me, and I will show you!" Your five senses (sight, smell, taste, touch, and feeling) are all sensory inputs for your brain to process data. Your brain takes the data, recognizes the environment, processes it, then you develop an awareness (something that is new) or an understanding of the now (familiarization of what you already know).

Notice the *object* of what you need to focus your trust on. And notice the object not to focus on that you will use to place your trust. In other words, you can't trust God with your mind, reasoning, or your own understand because everything that God does is far above what you could ever imagine. For example, we live on a planet and the universe that is governed by time. We can understand a beginning and an ending to things. We have accepted that not everything lasts forever. God reigns in an area where time doesn't exist. In other words, He never had a beginning because He always existed. He will never have an ending because He will always exist. Again, too deep to logically comprehend with your mind. So you must trust Him in your spirit in faith.

Every step that you take, regardless of what you see, regardless of what happens to you, around you, or to others, you must trust Him in faith. Acknowledging God means that you know that He is with you wherever you go, and you verbally say out loud that you are trusting Him in whatever situation that arises. I had to learn to practice putting Him first in everything, even down to how much money to spend on gasoline for my car. You may say, "Why on earth would you do that? Don't you know how much you need? Or just squeeze the gasoline pump handle until you hear *click* to indicate that the tank is full." I am not saying that I don't have confidence in how much money to spend on gasoline. I am training my mind and my spirit to be sensitive to God. I want to be able to hear His voice in anything, so I practice at the pump. I patiently wait until I hear a dollar amount to spend. I sometimes say out loud, "Lord, I heard this amount. I just want to be sure this is what You want me to do." And then I hear Him say, "Yes, that is the amount!"

When you give God your trust, He will direct your life.

Picture by Nicholas Gonzalez, Pexels.

12

> **Therefore I say to you, whatever things you ask when you pray, believe that you receive them, and you will have them.**
> **—Mark 11:24 (NKJV)**

I have heard so many Christians misuse this scripture, thinking that they can ask anything (and I mean anything) and they will automatically get it. Don't misunderstand my intentions. God can do anything, and He doesn't mind you having anything if it is aligned with His Word. As long as you are in line with His Word, you have a heart of a steward, and you are asking according to His will, then God promises to grant you the desires of your heart. What if God gives you something, you enjoy it for a couple of years, then suddenly He tells you to give it away? What will you do? My point is that if you are truly a steward, you know that whatever God gives you belongs to Him.

Jesus just walked by a fig tree that he cursed the day before. Peter said to Jesus, "Rabbi, look! The fig tree that you cursed has withered!" Then Jesus tells the disciples that if you have *faith* in God, you can say to a mountain to be cast into the sea. But here is the kicker: Whatever things that you ask when you pray, believe that you receive them, and you will have them. So my question to you is this: what did Jesus say that you will have? Everyone usually says you will have whatever things you ask. Maybe reflect on the scripture in James 4:2–3, which says, "You have not because you ask not." But look again at the scripture above. What *exactly* did Jesus say that you will have? This is not a trick question. Here is the answer: Jesus said you will have *whatever you believe that you receive when you pray!* You can pray for a lot of things, but if you don't believe that you have received them, then you are not using faith. This is so very important! You may say, "I don't understand. The whole reason why I'm praying for something is because I don't have it in my possession now." Remember the story of the centurion who went to Jesus asking Him to heal his servant. Jesus said He would come to his servant's home to heal him. But the centurion recognized Jesus's authority and said that he was not worthy for Jesus to come to his home. Pay attention to this. He said, "But only speak a word, and my servant will be healed." He was saying, "Jesus, if You speak his healing now, then my servant will be healed now!" He *believed* that he received his servant's healing now!

You may ask, "But I still struggle in that area. How do you do the faith thing?" Well, guess what. You do it all the time when you are ordering something online using your computer. Let's say you order a couch. When you're done with the order, you are given an invoice showing proof that you placed an order. Sometimes you print out your invoice just so that you can tell others that your couch is on the way. So is the couch physically in your house? Not yet. But you are already telling folks about your couch. In fact, you are even saying, "My couch," while believing that you have received it now. But the couch is not there yet. It is on the way. What is your proof that the couch is yours? The invoice! Guess what. Faith is your invoice! It is your proof of what you prayed for is on the way.

Picture by Pexels, Pixabay.

13

**For with man this is impossible, but
with God All things are possible.
—Matthew 19:26 (NKJV)**

There was a young man who was very wealthy who heard about the wonderful things that Jesus was doing. He had heard about how Jesus was healing people and how He was teaching people here and there. He finally concluded that Jesus was not only a great teacher but a person who knew the answer to what many people ask and are seeking. He wanted to know how to get into eternal life. But here is something that is extremely important: he asked Jesus what he must *do* to get into eternal life.

Jesus not only knew the answer, but He knew what the rich young ruler was thinking, which is common among everyone. What works must I do so that I can earn the right to enter eternal life? When Jesus responded to him, He guided him to the original Ten Commandments. And the young ruler quickly said, "Oh yes, yes! I'm doing that! I've been doing that ever since I was a child. What else (works) am I still missing?" Then Jesus threw a curve ball at him, saying, "If you want to be perfect, go sell what you have, give it to the poor, and you will have treasure in heaven. Come and follow me." The curveball is not a new commandment law. In fact, the scripture can be found in Leviticus 19:18. Out of the 613 commandment laws found in the Old Testament (Torah), Jesus asks the rich ruler regarding six laws, but then addresses something that was close to his heart. He knew that it is easy for man to follow some rules, but that is like following a checklist in your mind. Your heart is where your spirit is. It is *who* you are. You can do things to outwardly show others kindness, but inwardly your motives can be far different.

Jesus was trying to tell the rich ruler and His disciples that there is nothing you can do to be perfect enough to earn your way into eternal life. That is why Jesus came. *Everyone needs a Savior!* Jesus lived a perfect life and is the only one who is worthy to be a sacrifice to pay for our sin. Now when you reread the verse "for with man, it is impossible," Jesus was telling His disciples, "It is impossible for man to enter into eternal life alone based on his works. But God can do anything. And He has found a way to allow you into eternal life." God makes possible what is impossible!

Picture by Pexels, Pixabay.

14

**Call to Me, and I will answer you, and show you great and mighty things, which you do not know.
—Jeremiah 33:3 (NKJV)**

In DC Comic Books, there is a popular character that most people love called Superman. He was a person who came from the planet Krypton and was endowed with super capabilities powered from the earth's sun. When Clark Kent (Superman's undercover disguise) got a job working for the *Daily Planet* as a news reporter, he became friends with Jimmy Olson, a younger news reporter who carried around a camera taking pictures for the newspaper.

Every now and then, when Superman was saving Lois Lane from danger, Jimmy Olson was also around. Although Superman worked with Jimmy and Lois Lane in the office as Clark Kent, none of them knew who he really was. Some of you may not remember, but Superman gave Jimmy Olson a special wristwatch that emits an ultrahigh frequency that only Superman could hear. If Jimmy ever got in danger, he could press a button on his watch and Superman would come crashing through a wall to save him.

We have the same thing, and all we must do is just use our voices to call on the name of our Lord. God is never too busy to respond to you. He is beyond Superman. He is omniscient (all-knowing), omnipresent (everywhere), and omnipotent (all-powerful). There is no other being like Him. God loves us more than we will ever know, and there is nothing that can separate us from His Love for us.

Sometimes when we are in trouble and there is panic or fear surrounding us, we will yeah out, "Oh God!" or "Oh Lord!" But those words have become common, routine words without meaning. It is just a cliché (an overused word that lacks any deep thought). God is real. He is a person. He created you. He knows you. And He can do the impossible! It is OK to call on Him, saying, "Lord, I need You right now!"

Picture by James Wheeler, Pexels.

15

**Commit your works to the Lord, And your thoughts will be established.
—Proverbs 16:3 (NKJV)**

You know the word *commit* is such a scary word to some folks. Most young guys are frightened by that word when they hear it from a girl they are dating and the girl wants a monogamous relationship. When you look up the definition of the word *commit*, the Oxford definition explains the meaning as to carry out a pledge. The word *commit* also is found in the word *commitment*, which is tied to an obligation. The act of committing is connected to a person's character. In other words, if a person is committed to something, places action behind what he or she said, and gets the results they were looking for, then you would say that this person is of good character. Or this person is of good integrity because whatever they say they will do; you see the action or commitment behind the words.

When you research the word *commit* in the Hebrew language, it comes from the word *galal*, which means "to roll" (i.e., to roll away, to roll down, or to roll together). Thinking like an engineer, whenever you roll something, you think of something that is round or spherical like a rock. No matter how big the item is, if you keep rolling, you will experience a full 360-degree turn of the object. But then I started thinking about how you make a snowball. You first start with a small ball, and then you roll the snowball on the ground, adding more snow. As you continue to roll (commit), to add more snow (work), your snowball will get larger and larger.

Jesus mentions to His disciples in John 15:7 that if they abide in Him (living and dwelling in Him), and His words abide (living and dwelling) in them, (meaning they are doing the things, the works that He is telling them to do), then whatever they ask will be done for them. I like that! Let me repeat. Whatever you ask that you desire will be done for you! You don't have to work out the part that is for you. It will be done for you!

Don't misunderstand this scripture as doing works in order to guarantee your salvation. After you become a Christian, we do good works in love to spread the gospel to others, to help others, and to minister to others as God leads us. By following His will, and doing His work, God is saying, "Because I love you so very much, and because I know what is in your heart, I will also include granting you your desires!" God knows your thoughts! He knows what makes you happy! So by giving yourself solely unto Him, He promises to lead and guide you into areas that will fulfill your every desire.

Picture by Pille Kirsi, Pexels.

16

**The Lord will work out his plans for my life—for your faithful love, O Lord, endures forever.
—Psalm 138:8 (NLT)**

Did you know that God has a specific plan for every human being who was born on this planet? You were not only just the result of a male and female human being getting together and creating a baby. A male and female can create the biology cells to create another human being. But the human spirit comes from God.

Now I know you are wondering, *Why are there some evil people on this earth? Are you saying that God created evil people and He is to blame for the evil that is going on in this world?* To answer your questions, no. God does create the human spirit, but He gives everyone a free will and free choice to choose what path in life that they want. In fact, you don't have to follow God, Jesus Christ, the Holy Spirit, or have anything to do with Christianity. God will literally allow you to live your life. But at the end of your life, you will be separated from Him because He created the heavens and the earth. You will be separated from everything that is good and everything that involves love.

Satan's plan for you is to keep you distracted from knowing what God's plan is for your life. Why? Well, here are a few reasons:

1. He hates you! Don't ever think that Satan is your friend because you came from God and you were created in the image of God. When Satan sees you, he sees the image

of God and he hates God because he was removed from his position in heaven, and will eventually be permanently kicked out of heaven! (See Revelation 12:7–9) Jesus told His disciples that He saw Satan and his demons fall from heaven like lightning.
2. Satan wants your witness to others to be tarnished and ineffective. God's plan for your life is to help with His redemption plan of telling others about Jesus Christ so that they can accept Him, receive forgiveness of their sins, and enter heaven.
3. Satan wants you to give up hope that God loves you or God has turned His back on you.
4. Satan wants you to miss out on the treasures, rewards, and crowns that are in heaven.

But if you choose to follow God, or you are seeking Him, then He has a plan for you. It is a wonderful plan, and by staying close to Him, He promises to help guide you to your destiny.

Picture by Joe Calomeni, Pexels.

17

My grace is sufficient for you, for My strength is made perfect in weakness.
—2 Corinthians 12:9 (NKJV)

By now you are realizing that the Christian walk is not an easy journey. Jesus never said that when we follow Him that all of our problems will go away. To be truthful, Jesus clearly said that "in this world you will have tribulation, but be of good cheer, because He has overcome the world" (John 16:33). He also said that the world (the people in the world and how things operate) will hate you because the world hated Him first (John 15:18)! But you need to know that Jesus did not leave us without provisions and help.

Why does God allow things to happen to us? Because He wants you to have faith in Him. If nothing bad ever happens to you, you will never need faith. When Lazarus was sick, Jesus could have rushed over to the city of Bethany to heal him. But Jesus said something very, *very* powerful that a lot of folks miss. Jesus said, "This sickness is not unto death, but for the glory of God" (John 11:4). Jesus didn't say that Lazarus was not going to die. He was saying that this sickness was not going to end with death; there is another chapter after the death. Jesus knew that Lazarus was going to die and used the circumstance to show others what God can do to instill faith and belief in the people to trust in God. Jesus even waited an extra two days after Lazarus died before going to see him. He walked two miles to get to the body of Lazarus. We he arrived, He told the people that He was the resurrection and the life. So when He instructed them to roll away the stone from the tomb, Martha (Lazarus's sister) was trying to tell Jesus that Lazarus had been dead for four days now and his body was starting to stink! But Jesus corrected her by saying, "Did I not say to you that if you would believe you would see the Glory of God?" People are paralyzed when it comes to a person who has been dead for four days. Jesus was trying to get them to see that it was His strength that was going to raise Lazarus from the tomb *if* they believed in Him.

God gives you His grace not for you to hoard, gloat, and get all puffed up with pride to say, "OK, Lord, I can do all things. I got it from here!" The weaker you are, the stronger He is, as long as you are believing, trusting, and having faith in Him. God's grace is not for you, but it works through you so that it will help others. God's grace and His blessing are always meant to help someone else so that others will start to believe in Him.

Picture by Michael Steinberg, Pexels.

18

I will give you the treasures of darkness And hidden riches of secret places, That you may know that I, the Lord, Who call you by your name.
—Isaiah 45:3 (NKJV)

I know many pastors, people in the ministry, and other Christians who have taken scriptures similar to this and pulled them out of context. In other words, they are looking at it through the eyes of selfish motives, looking at what they deserve as opposed to what God wants them to do with the wealth. God already knows that every person wants to be prosperous and not live in poverty. But He cares more about what you do with the wealth. Are you using wealth to just buy stuff for yourself, or are you using it to help others? God knows the desires of your heart, and He wants you to have the best of the best. But He doesn't want the stuff to have the best of you. In fact, *anything* (any object) that is between you and God, you will begin to give more attention to and in effect worship. Worship is giving attention to, giving allegiance, honor, and acknowledgment of its worth to something. And worshipping things is called idolatry.

Here is something to remember: Satan will tempt you with things, but God will test you with things. A temptation is when the object you desire will only benefit you. It is a desire for things for selfish gain. When God tests you, it is usually a sacrifice that will benefit Him or benefit others. God *loves* to bless you with things to make you happy. But if later He tells you to give it away to someone else, will you do it? That is the test. Are you so greedy that you will hide it and keep it for yourself? Your attitude and behavior toward things reveal whether you are a servant of God or just living for yourself.

God wants your obedience. And He is the one who gives you the ability to obtain wealth. God wants you to prosper and be in good health as your soul prospers. What good is it to give a person a ton of money and their mind is the most corrupt and evil character that exists? Notice at the end of the above scripture that there is reminder of the one who made you wealthy! The motive of God making you wealthy is so that it reminds you that it was Him who made you wealthy.

Live with a heart of thanksgiving and gratitude.

Picture by Michael Leland, Pexels.

19

**Thy word have I hid in mine heart, that
I might not sin against thee.
—Psalm 119:11 (KJV)**

When folks read this scripture, they acknowledge that it is a good scripture, but they fail to understand its importance. While growing up, I heard many elderly folks say this scripture, but it came across as something poetic instead of something instructional that we need to do.

Imagine you are in the military and your drill sergeant has given you a brand-new semiautomatic rifle that is extremely powerful. So powerful that one squeeze of the trigger is guaranteed to take down your enemy. The sergeant tells you that you need to take the time to study this new rifle, read the instructions, and learn everything you can about it because it will save your life on the battlefield. Weeks and months go by and you haven't read the manual on the weapon. You glance through the manual every now and then but never take the time to study it in detail. One day you get deployed to fight. After a long trip, you are in a helicopter and you are getting ready to jump using your rope to get to the ground. After you land safely on the ground, you immediately start running toward your enemy. Now you are thinking, *OK, I got this new awesome rifle that can defeat my enemy!* But you haven't taken the time to study how it works! So the only thing you know how to do is to start running toward the enemy yelling, "Hoorah!" and waving the rifle in the air! How effective will you be? You may look like you can defeat the enemy, but you haven't loaded the rifle, pushed the right buttons, released the safety, and pulled the trigger. In fact, you might be pulling the trigger and just hearing *click click click* while you're running toward the enemy!

So many Christians place their Bibles on the nightstand assuming that the Holy Spirit is going to transfer *everything* they need to know into their brains so that it is available when they need it. It doesn't work that way. Remember this: The Holy Spirit pulls out of you the scriptures (God's Word) that you have put inside of you. As you study and read the Word of God (putting the Word inside of you), you are building up your arsenal of bullets so that when the enemy comes, the Holy Spirit will load up your weapon (your mind), so that you can pull the trigger (speak the Word) and defeat the enemy.

The Word of God is like seed. Seed is of no benefit to you if it isn't planted in good soil. It is our responsibility to plant (make the effort to read and study God's Word) His Word in our spirits (good soil), so that it will take root and grow. When God's Word starts to grow in your spirit, the Holy Spirit begins to bring to your memory the things that you planted so that it will be helpful to you!

The Word of God is also your weapon when you are fighting against demonic enemies, and using God's Word is the key to defeating them. We must remember that we are in *spiritual warfare*, and you must use *spiritual weapons*. Speaking God's Word is the key to not only pulling the trigger, but impacting your circumstances that surrounds you.

Picture by Ron Cobbs.

20

**Have I not commanded you? Be strong and of good courage; do not be afraid, nor be dismayed, for the Lord your God is with you wherever you go.
—Joshua 1:9 (NKJV)**

Joshua and Caleb were two of the original children of Israel who walked on dry land when God parted the Red Sea, and they were there when the Ten Commandments were given. They were the only two men who trusted and believed in God when they saw the land of Canaan; in spite of seeing giants walking around in the land, they told Moses, "We can take the land!" Because of such negativity that spread among the people, God was angry and forced the children of Israel to roam through the desert for forty years until the original children died in the desert. Only the descendants of the children of Israel were allowed to go into the Promised Land. Even Moses wasn't allowed into the Promised Land because of his failure to obey God in one area.

After Moses died, the huge task of leading over a million people into the Promised Land fell on the shoulders of Joshua. God came to Joshua and got directly to the point. "Moses, My servant, is dead, but get up and go to the Promised Land that I have given to you." God was telling Joshua that the same way He was with Moses, He will be with him. God knew that there will be situations that are scary and doubtful. But He was reminding Joshua that He would be with him wherever he would go. Keep in mind that Joshua was around the age of eighty when God told him to lead the children of Israel.

There are many times we feel the same way. God is always with you, even when you don't feel like He is there. Since the time we were born, we have trusted and relied on our human senses and what we can reason and understand. God is not limited to our human senses, and He is far above our reasoning and understanding. This one scripture focuses on three words: belief, trust, and faith. If you don't have those three words active in your spirit and in your mind, then fear, doubt, and unbelief reign in your mind and spirit. It is the opposite of what God is asking you to do! (The opposite of belief is unbelief. The opposite of trust is doubt. And the opposite of faith is the combination of unbelief and doubt, which leads to emotion of fear.)

And the same goes for you. God's ways are the same (Malachi 3:6). God promises to be with you. God promises to never leave you or forsake you. God wants you to believe in Him, trust Him, and have faith in Him in everything that you do and in everything He asks you to do.

Picture by Hugo Sykes, Pexels.

21

Fear not, for I am with you; Be not dismayed, for I am your God. I will strengthen you, yes, I will help you, I will uphold you with My righteous right hand.
—Isaiah 41:10 (NKJV)

Have you ever been afraid? I'm not talking about when you were a child. I'm talking about even now as an adult you get afraid. A lot of people were afraid of the COVID-19 virus because in the beginning, there was no medical vaccine to fight against this virus. Yes, I do understand that a lot of folks opposed taking the vaccine, but my point is that this virus was and is a killer. But the same is true in getting cancer. Some folks are afraid of losing all of their money due to identity theft and cyber criminals. With so much evil going on in the world, it is very hard to even want to step out of your house to just live.

Jesus said that we would go through tribulation. Fear and anxiety arise when you are telling yourself in your mind that you don't know what to do. In fact, your mind is thinking about the what-ifs. What if this happens and you don't have an answer or don't know what to do? That is when your mind is flooded with fear, anxiety, then folks start having panic attacks. *Panic attacks are fueled by fear and anxiety.* Your mind is spiraling in a never-ending cycle of what-ifs. I need to do something, but I don't know what to do! Then the next what-if pops into your mind because you are thinking about the consequence of how bad it is going to get.

God sees everything and knows everything. There is nothing that is a surprise to God. God has a solution to any and everything that arises because He knows and sees the future. God always responds when you have faith in Him. He gives you the strength that you need to endure and get through your troubles. Remember He gives you the strength you need.

God knows that as you go through life, the things that you experience can appear to be frightening. But be of good cheer. God is on your side, and He promises to not let you fall, to keep you moving forward, and to bring your through whatever trials you are going through.

Picture by Rodolfo, Pexels.

22

**Casting all your care upon Him, for He cares for you.
—1 Peter 5:7 (NKJV)**

A long time ago, I heard a sermon that gave the illustration of what most Christians do when they read this scripture. They go to the altar or wherever they pray with a bag full of their troubles, problems, and griefs believing that God hears them. After placing the bag down, they are praying up a storm—sweating, pleading to God, crying, shouting, and doing everything they can think of to make sure God heard them. After they finish praying, they get up off their knees, pick up the bag of issues and problems, and go back with their problems wondering why I don't see a difference? In other words, they have said the prayer, but they truly haven't given their problems over to the Lord.

I heard another pastor use the example of a fishing rod and reel. While holding the rod, you move it back behind your shoulder then quickly move the rod in front of you to cause the bait on the line to shoot far away from you into the water. The only problem with that analogy is that it still relates to the previous example because over time, you are still reeling the bait (problems) back to you! When you look up the word *cast* in Greek, it literally means to throw! When you reread the scripture using the word *throw*, you will get the full meaning and intent of what God is telling you. Throw all of your cares (worries and anxieties) upon Him, for He cares for you! When you throw something away, you don't go running after it to pick it up again. You are giving your worries to the Lord!

Here is an example of how you give your worries and anxieties to the Lord:

> Dear Heavenly Father, this problem that I'm facing is overwhelming my mind and starting to steal my joy. Your Word says that if I cast and throw all of my worries and anxieties to You, that You will care for me. In fact, You cared for me even before the problems ever entered my life. Father, from this point forward, I give all my worries to You. I don't understand what to do, I don't know what to do, and I don't know how this will get done or go away. But I trust You, Lord. I have faith in You, Lord. I choose not to take back the anxieties that I have given to You. And I know that all things work out for the good to those who are called to Your purpose. I thank You and believe that I receive Your peace of mind, right now. In the name of Jesus I pray! Amen.

When you pray this, I guarantee that the enemy will place thoughts in your mind about the problem you were worrying over. You must remind the enemy that he needs to talk to God about it because you have given all your worries to Him! Resist the devil, and he will flee.

Picture by Rodolfo, Pexels.

23

**For God did not give us the spirit of fear,
but of Love, Power, and a Sound Mind.
—2 Timothy 1:7 (NKJV)**

All fear does not come from God because fear is a spirit. God is a spirit and God is love. There is no fear in God. God is omnipotent, and there is no other being, creature, or god that is more powerful than Him.

Whenever you feel afraid, you must remember that the presence of fear is not of God. In fact, by thinking negative thoughts, and speaking negative things, you give permission to the devil to bring about the things that can harm you. The Old Testament speaks of Job talking out loud about the things that he feared the most and the things he dreaded that happened to him. Just by speaking the thoughts that the enemy has placed in your mind gives him permission to do unto you what you dread. Think about all the negative things that have happened to you. Could you be the one who opened the door for the enemy to inflict these things on you?

God is the one who gives you love, power, and a sound mind. Why do you need a sound mind? So that you know what to do. Depression is the lack of hope. It is constantly thinking that there is no way out. There is a scripture in Proverbs that says, "Hope deferred makes the heart sick." Without hope, your spirit is very weak. So if the enemy can take your mind off hope, and to constantly worry and be afraid, then it makes you weak and sick. Here is a secret: Did you know that worry is constantly thinking about future events that have not happened yet? Think about it. You are thinking about what might happen. But you live in the present. The future event has not happened yet, and that is what you are worrying about. God can see your future. He can change it, send along help when you get to that point, or equip you with the strength to endure and overcome whenever it comes.

When a negative thought comes to your mind, you immediately need to throw it out of your mind. Don't misunderstand that God will use the Holy Spirit to remind or warn you of things. But it is never to invoke fear. In fact, when you read the Bible, practically everywhere there is an angel or a message from God. The first thing said is "Fear not."

King David said it clearly when he wrote the twenty-third chapter in the book of Psalms. "Although I walk through the valley of the shadow of death, I will fear no evil. For you are with me." David knew that fear was only a shadow. And shadows can't hurt you. It doesn't say that the object of harm doesn't exist. It is just saying don't be afraid of it because you have the Greater One with you!

Live in faith in God.

Conclusion

I strongly encourage you to commit these scriptures to memory. These twenty-three power scriptures will *knock down barriers, open closed doors,* and create *peace of mind* that will enable you to endure and live a better life on this earth. Getting God's Word inside you and speaking His Word out loud was the key. Throughout my life, I read the Word and knew the Word, meaning, I heard the Word before. I even had them highlighted in my Bible. But I never knew the importance of speaking the Word over my life daily. Reading God's Word is *logos* (knowledge). It feeds your brain with information. But speaking God's Word is known as rhema! You are using air out of your lungs to voice the Word of God into existence. You can say things all day long. You may have good intentions, but sometimes things don't happen. But God's Word never comes back void. When you speak His Word from the Bible, it must take action. God's words are so powerful that heaven and earth can pass away and end, but His Word will never pass away!

As always, I asked the Lord to help me memorize these scriptures. He gave me this idea, and it really works. Write down each scripture on a three-inch-by-five-inch card. You can even personalize the scripture so that when you are saying them out loud you are speaking the affirmation. For example, when you write 1 Peter 5:7, you can say, "Casting all of my cares (worries, problems, and anxieties) upon the Lord because He cares about me!" After you have written down all of the scriptures on a three-inch-by-five-inch card, place them where you will see them every day. I taped mine to my bathroom mirror. As I'm getting dressed in the morning, I read those scriptures out loud! Take your time as you read them. Over time, you will begin to memorize the scriptures, but it is a lot easier to remember them after you have personalized them.

If you don't know Jesus Christ as your Lord and personal Savior, I invite you to ask Him into your life. If you were to die right now, you were in front of the pearly gates of heaven, and God asked you, "Why should I let you in?" what would you say? If you say that you were a good person and you've done a lot of good things in your life, that may be true, but God is a Holy God. If you have ever done one thing wrong, then there needs to be payment for that wrong. The Bible says that all have sinned and fallen short (Romans 3:23). And the wage (payment) of sin is death (total separation from God for all eternity; Romans 6:23). But God has a backup plan. He knew that everyone in the world was not perfect. His backup plan was to send Jesus to make the payment for you. Jesus was born on this earth, lived a perfect life, was hung on the cross, and God placed every sin that humankind could ever take on His Son Jesus Christ. God took out his wrath, anger, and punishment on Jesus so that we didn't have to take that punishment. And now, He is giving us eternal life through faith. If you believe in Jesus (confess with your mouth that Jesus is your Lord, believe in your heart that He took the punishment for you by dying on the cross, and God raised Him from the dead), then you will be saved from God's punishment (Romans 10:9–10). You are saved by grace that God gives to you through your faith in believing in Jesus Christ. You can't work or earn your way into heaven (Ephesians 2:8). God's grace is free! It is a free gift!

> God loves you so very much, that He sent His Son to pay the price that you couldn't afford to pay. All you need to do is believe on Him, and God will give you eternal life. (John 3:16)

Notes

Notes